ANIMALS IN THE WILD

MALAYAN TAPIR

Annette Whipple

A Crabtree Forest Book

Crabtree Publishing
crabtreebooks.com

Notes for Readers and Class Discussion

This book is designed to teach readers about core subject areas, build curiosity, and inspire further investigation. Readers are encouraged to build upon what they already know about the subject and engage in topics they want to learn more about. Here are a few guiding questions to prompt reflection and discussion. Possible answers appear in red.

Before Reading:

Read the title and look at the table of contents. What do you already know about Malayan tapirs?

- *I know that Malayan tapirs have long snouts that they use to grab food.*
- *I know that Malayan tapirs are herbivores, meaning that they eat mainly plants.*

What would you like to learn about Malayan tapirs?

- *I would like to learn about the habitats where Malayan tapirs live.*
- *I would like to learn whether the Malayan tapir is endangered.*

During Reading:

Pause after reading each page or chapter. What questions do you have about what you read? What are you curious to know?

- *I am curious to know why the Malayan tapir has feet with both toes and hooves.*
- *I wonder why the digestive juices of the Malayan tapir's stomach help some seeds to germinate faster than if they hadn't been eaten.*

Make connections to what you are reading. How is this like something you already know?

- *I know that some animals, such as the star-nosed mole and the giant anteater, have unique noses that help them find food in their habitats.*
- *I know that some animals, such as hippos and rhinos, have thick, tough skin that helps protect them against predators.*

After Reading:

Recall key details about the book. What was the author trying to teach readers?

- *The author was trying to teach readers about the characteristics, behaviors, and habitats of Malayan tapirs.*
- *The author was trying to teach readers that Malayan tapirs are an endangered species and at risk of becoming extinct if they are not protected.*

How did the images and captions help you understand more?

- *The photographs helped to show me what the Malayan tapir looks like in its environment.*
- *The captions helped me understand new details about Malayan tapirs.*

Table of Contents

Meet the Malayan Tapir

What Asian animal has a pig-shaped body, a long **snout**, and hair similar in color to a giant panda? It's the Malayan tapir! It's also known as the Asian or Indian tapir.

Mountain Tapir

Baird's Tapir

Asia's Tapir

Tapirs are plant-eating animals that look like a cross between a horse and a rhinoceros. There are four tapir **species**: mountain, lowland, Baird's, and Malayan. Of the four, only Malayan tapirs live in Asia. The mountain tapir, Baird's tapir, and Malayan tapir are all **endangered**. Scientists consider the lowland tapir a **vulnerable** species as its population is decreasing.

Lowland Tapir

Mammals

Malayan tapirs are mammals. All mammals share some of the same characteristics. They keep a constant body temperature even as their environment gets warmer or colder. Hair or fur covers their skin. Females give birth to live young and feed their young with the milk the mother produces.

Chapter 1

What Do They Look Like?

Malayan tapirs grow to be quite large. These sturdy animals have **prehistoric**-looking heads, thick bodies, and stumpy legs.

Malayan tapirs have white hair on their ears. Their eyesight is poor so they rely a lot on their keen sense of smell.

Malayan tapirs are the largest of the tapir species.

As Big as a Couch

Malayan tapirs can be 6 to 8 feet (1.8 to 2.4 m) long—that's around the length of a couch. When on all fours, they stand nearly 4 feet (1.2 m) tall at the shoulders. These mammals can weigh more than 720 pounds (330 kg), or about as much as a pair of lions.

Dramatic Coloring

The coloring of a Malayan tapir is unique. Its head, neck, and four legs are black. Its thick middle is white or gray. The dramatic coloring makes the Malayan tapir memorable. But more importantly, this saddle-shaped pattern of coloring provides **camouflage** in shady forests.

Built for Speed

The large, stocky bodies of Malayan tapirs move with surprising speed. Their feet have both toes and hooves. When threatened, tapirs often outrun potential **predators**. They crash through the dense forest **vegetation** to safety.

Long Snout

Notice the snout of a Malayan tapir. It is long and flexible—like a short elephant trunk. The tapir's nose and upper lip extend to create this prehensile snout. Prehensile means the snout grabs and wraps around things. Malayan tapirs use their snouts to pluck leaves from trees and fruits from the ground while **foraging**. When they dive deep in water, their snouts act like a **snorkel**. The nostrils close so water doesn't get in their lungs.

Other animals that have long, flexible snouts include the aardvark, which uses its snout to find insects to eat.

Keen Sniffers

Of all their senses, a Malayan tapir's sense of smell is the most important. It sniffs along forest trails for **scent markings**. A tapir sprays urine, or pee, along forest paths to leave scent marks behind. Then it sniffs its way from a feeding area to a water source along the familiar path. Scent markings can also be left as a message to other tapirs.

Many Toes

Malayan tapirs have 14 toes. Each front foot, or forefoot, has four toes each. The back feet have three toes. The middle toe is larger than the other toes and bears the most weight. Their toes help them easily climb steep riverbanks and slopes. They even scramble over barriers. Their toes give them extra traction in slippery mud and on river bottoms.

Tapirs use their snouts for pulling plants and placing them in their mouths.

Each of the Malayan tapir's toes ends in a small hoof.

Chapter 2

Home and Habitat

Malayan tapirs live in Southeast Asia in the countries of Thailand, Myanmar, Malaysia, and Indonesia. They are forest dwellers, but can also be found in open fields.

Broad Range

Malayan tapirs have been observed near villages and even outside of major cities. They sometimes leave their forest **habitat** in search of food. Their range in the wild extends from southern Thailand and southern Myanmar through Malaysia. They also live on the Indonesian island of Sumatra.

The Malayan tapir's habitat includes lowland tropical swamps and hill forests.

Forest Animals

The rainforests and drier forests along lower mountain slopes are the Malayan tapir's traditional habitat. They prefer lower **elevations** and valleys. These animals also spend time at forest edges, and sometimes open fields. They may also make their homes in new forests that have grown back after being logged.

Close to Home

Malayan tapirs don't travel far each day. Biologists have recorded them walking less than one-quarter of a mile (0.32 km) in a day, which is about the length of a city block. Sometimes they walk up to 2.5 miles (4 km). Over time, they may wander farther—but always within a specific range.

Solitary Animals

Malayan tapirs typically have home range territories of 4 to 10 square miles (10–25 sq. km). Their ranges can overlap with the ranges of other tapirs—but they prefer to be alone. Females usually have larger home ranges than males. Malayan tapirs move to different forests as needed. They often move to avoid forest fires and to find food when it's scarce.

Some Malayan tapirs in Malaysia live within 3 miles (5 km) of some of the country's major cities and villages. Sometimes they have to be rescued from wells they have fallen into while searching for water.

Water Babies

Malayan tapirs spend a lot of time in marshes and rivers. They are excellent swimmers and divers. These mammals completely submerge under water. Using their snorkel-like snouts they stay under water for several minutes, walking along the mud of the river bottom.

Tapirs often wallow in muddy areas to cool off and avoid being bitten by insects.

Researchers have found that Malayan tapirs like to live within close range of a salt lick. These are mineral deposits where animals lick sodium, calcium, and other minerals they need for bone and muscle growth.

Ecosystem Restorers

Scientists say Malayan tapirs help restore unhealthy rainforests. They do this by spreading more seeds, through their poop, in **deforested** areas than in healthy forests. This makes Malayan tapirs natural habitat rebuilders. They are key to restoring **ecosystems** destroyed by deforestation.

Chapter 3

What to Eat?

Malayan tapirs are herbivores, which means they feed on plants. They find most of their food in the variety of vegetation that grows in the forest understory.

Seeds, Buds, and Shoots

Malayan tapirs eat lots of seeds, leaves, soft twigs, and buds. Fruits and leaves that fall to the forest floor are also devoured. They consume tree bark, shrubs, and **succulents**. Since they spend so much time in water, tapirs also eat aquatic plants.

Called "selective browsers," Malayan tapirs mainly prefer the young leaves and shoots of plants.

Finding Food

Malayan tapirs consume more than 100 kinds of plants, and feed in a variety of forest and swamp locations. They zigzag from plant to plant. Tapirs prefer high-quality food when it's available. They eat a variety of fruits.

Malayan tapirs like to eat foods such as figs and palm fruits.

Flexible Snout

A flexible snout is vital for a Malayan tapir's survival. This animal forages for plants by sniffing. It then plucks leaves from trees and the ground. The tapir moves the food to its mouth with its flexible snout. When a small tree has leaves which are out of reach, the sturdy animal walks over it until the tree bends or breaks. Then the tapir eats the vegetation it wants.

In Malaysia, the Malayan tapir is known to eat more than 115 species of forest plants.

Seed Germinators

Malayan tapirs eat a lot of fruits with seeds. They spit out some seeds, but swallow many. Most seeds pass through the tapir's **digestive system** whole. The digestive juices of the tapir's stomach help some seeds **germinate** faster than if they hadn't been eaten.

Malayan tapirs are considered a keystone species. These are animals that have a large impact on their ecosystem. If they die out, it can cause the ecosystem to collapse.

Food Conflict

In fringe areas near farmlands, Malayan tapirs are known to bend and break rubber trees while foraging for the leaves and stems they want. This causes conflict with farmers. The farmers often want to rid their territories of Malayan tapirs through trapping and hunting.

Durian fruit is a favorite of Malayan tapirs in Sumatra. This tropical fruit is known for its terrible rotten-flesh smell.

Environmental Adaptations

Malayan tapirs are the only living Asian species of tapirs. They are believed to have **evolved** from a species found in North America 50 million years ago. They **migrated** and **adapted** to their environments over millions of years. In different areas of Asia, these animals eat slightly different foods. In Sumatra, for example, they eat leaves, shoots, flowers, and fruits from breadfruit and other trees, succulent plants, and mosses. In Thailand, they eat more leaves than fruits.

Chapter 4

Malayan Tapir Behavior

Adult Malayan tapirs prefer to spend most of their time alone. They come together to **mate**. Females then care for their young on their own.

When Malayan tapirs meet one another in the wild, they smell and touch one another. However, they often become aggressive, biting or chasing one another. They also mark their territory to warn off others.

Tapirs take long sniffs with their snouts.

Speedy Little Legs

Despite their stout bodies, Malayan tapirs are quite **agile**. They are good climbers and have quick bursts of speed. They swim and dive in water. They spend a great deal of time there eating aquatic plants, removing ticks from their skin, and cooling their bodies.

Malayan tapirs eat more in the evening.

Twilight Animals

Malayan tapirs aren't strictly active during one part of the day. Though awake during the day, they also have regular daytime sleep patterns. They're also active at night. But they seem to be most active at twilight, or dawn and dusk.

Many animals are more active during twilight, including coyotes, bears, rabbits, and skunks.

I'll Call You...

Although tapirs live alone, they do communicate with one another. Their squeaks are high-pitched. They whistle for different lengths of time and at different pitches. Malayan tapirs also make clicking sounds and hiccup-like noises. When they're scared or in pain, their sounds provide warning calls to others. They also vocalize when mating.

Malayan tapirs often have overlapping home ranges, so warning calls are important.

Smell You Later...

With their long snouts, Malayan tapirs have an acute sense of smell and rely on it to communicate. They spray urine on their favorite paths to leave scent messages called **pheromones**. Each tapir has its own unique scent. Malayan tapirs curl their lips to detect others' pheromones. This helps them understand the message better than just sniffing.

The Malayan tapir has a special organ on the roof of its mouth that allows it to better detect pheromones.

Chapter 5

The Next Generation

Malayan tapirs rely on pheromones to communicate about mating. These scent messages are how males and females introduce themselves to potential mates.

Malayan tapirs also curl their lips while mating to better smell one another.

Courtship

In the wild, female tapirs usually begin **breeding** at around three years old. Breeding season is in May and June. Males and females follow courtship rituals such as chasing and circling one another. They also sniff each other. Sometimes they bite. They often vocalize with whistles.

One at a Time

During the breeding season, adult Malayan tapirs are monogamous, meaning they only mate with one tapir. They also only breed every two years. Once mating occurs, females have a 13-month pregnancy. When ready to give birth, the female finds a safe place. Typically, only one calf at a time is born, with twins occurring rarely.

The mother licks her calf after it's born. She does this for many reasons, including to encourage the calf to stand.

Calves begin to eat solid foods at about two weeks old. They grow quickly.

Baby Tapirs

Like their distant relatives—horses—newborn Malayan tapir calves stand as soon as they can. This is often just hours after birth. A calf weighs about 15 pounds (7 kg). This is about as much as two human newborns. Reddish-brown hair covers its entire body. Young tapirs differ in appearance from their parents. Their white stripes and spots help them camouflage in sunlight and shadows.

A baby tapir's white stripes and spots keep them safe from predators when they are young. They fade at about six months.

Mother's Milk

The mother provides for all the newborn tapir's needs and protects it. The baby nurses two to three times a day. It also grows quickly. It begins to eat solid foods when it's about two weeks old. Malayan tapir calves swim at three weeks!

At about three weeks, a Malayan tapir calf can swim.

Life Cycle

The young tapir continues to change. Its spots and stripes begin to fade. At around six months old, the Malayan tapir has the black-and-white coloring of its mother. Around that same time, it **weans** from its mother, consuming plants of the forest for food.

Mother's Protection

The tapir continues to grow. It plays and learns about life as a Malayan tapir. A young tapir stays with its mother for 12–18 months before it lives on its own. It's ready to mate around three years of age. Malayan tapirs can live to 30 years of age.

Tapir calves often stay with their mothers until the next mating season and beyond.

Chapter 6

Malayan Tapir Conservation

Malayan tapirs have few natural predators. Their black-and-white coloring camouflages them in forest shadows. Their large size protects them from many animals. But their **conservation** status is endangered—due to human activity.

The Malayan tapir's thick, tough skin helps protect against the fangs of animals, as well as any sharp branches it brushes against when running through the forest.

Escape Artists

The Malayan tapir's speed often gets it to safety, as it can easily run to water and jump in. Only fast cats such as tigers and leopards naturally prey on these tapirs, but even that is rare. Malayan tapirs also have a powerful bite. Their tough skin is about 1 inch (2.5 cm) thick on their necks and heads.

Ecological Corridors

At one time, Malayan tapirs were hunted for meat. Hunting is forbidden now. But human–tapir interactions still cause problems. Tapirs are killed in road accidents. To cut down on roadkill, governments have introduced ecological corridors, or areas where protective measures such as speed-limit enforcement, wildlife crossings, solar lights, and signs are in place.

Deforestation

These animals have lost much of their habitat to deforestation. When forests are extensively logged for construction and industry, Malayan tapirs are left with habitats that are fragmented, or broken apart. This makes it difficult to breed and find food. Humans **encroach** on Malayan tapir territories to build homes and infrastructure such as roads and bridges.

Survival Plans

Scientists evaluate a lot of details to decide if an animal species needs help to survive. They look at:

- total population, and if the population is growing or decreasing
- natural habitat availability and how much is needed
- conservation efforts

Conservation in the wild is key to species survival.

Malayan tapirs are listed as endangered by the International Union for Conservation of Nature (IUCN) Red List. They have been on this list since 1986.

Conservation Work

As an endangered species, Malayan tapirs have a very high risk of **extinction** in the wild based on the threats they face. We know Malayan tapirs are in trouble. Without conservation efforts they will become extinct. Conservation includes changing human behaviors that threaten the animals. It also includes laws, directed programs, and breeding programs in zoos that increase their population.

Zoo breeding programs can help Malayan tapir populations survive so that they can one day be re-released into wild areas.

Role of Agriculture

Large-scale agriculture is a major threat to the forest habitat of Malayan tapirs. Many forests were destroyed to make way for palm oil **plantations**. Palm oil is an edible vegetable oil made from the fruit of the African oil palm tree. Thousands of these trees are planted on cleared forest land. This type of farming displaces wild animals, destroying their homes and the foods they normally eat.

Indonesia is the world's biggest producer of palm oil—with 60 percent of the world's production. Malaysia is the world's second-largest producer.

Protected Status

Conservation groups have pushed governments to protect forests. Palm oil manufacturers have made some changes. Now the biggest problem for tapirs is the loss of large forests due to illegal logging. Malayan tapirs are protected from international trade and hunting. The country of Malaysia began protecting tapirs in 1955.

Indonesia has protected Malayan tapirs since 1931. Malaysia has promised to save half of the country's forests.

Saving Malayan Tapirs

Scientists first recognized the need to protect Malayan tapirs nearly 100 years ago. Today, less than 2,500 Malayan tapirs live in the wild. Despite conservation efforts, Malayan tapirs are still endangered. They can be saved if governments truly commit to conservation. This requires that governments make strong protection laws while also funding habitat restoration.

Conservation groups such as Rainforest Action Network fund community-based action plans that help protect wild animals such as the Malayan tapir. These plans work with the people who live in and near Malayan tapir habitats.

adapt (uh-DAPT): To change a trait or behavior so that it is easier to live in a particular environment

agile (AJ-ahyl): Able to move quickly and easily

breeding (BREE-ding): Producing offspring

camouflage (KAM-uh-flahzh): Colors and patterns that help an animal blend in with its natural surroundings

conservation (kon-ser-VEY-shuhn): The protection of animals, plants, and their habitats

deforested (dee-FAWR-ist-ed): Cleared of large areas of trees

digestive system (dahy-JES-tiv SIS-tuhm): The set of organs in the body, including the stomach and intestines, that turns food into energy and nutrients

ecosystem (EE-koh-sis-tuhm): A community of living and nonliving things in their environment

elevation (el-uh-VEY-shuhn): The height of a place, usually measured above or below sea level

encroach (en-KROHCH): To gradually move into an area that is beyond the usual limits

endangered (en-DEYN-jerd): An animal or plant species that is considered to be at a very high risk of becoming extinct in the wild

evolved (ih-VOLVD): Changed gradually over a long period of time to survive better in an environment

extinction (ik-STINGK-shuhn): When an animal or plant species completely dies out and disappears from Earth forever

forage (FAWR-ij): To search for food

germinate (JUR-muh-neyt): To cause to sprout or develop

habitat (HAB-i-tat): The place where an animal or plant naturally lives and grows

mate (meyt): When a male and female animal join together for the purpose of producing offspring

migrate (MAHY-greyt): To move from one area to another at different times of the year

pheromone (FER-uh-mohn): A chemical substance that an animal produces to communicate with other animals of the same species

plantation (plan-TEY-shuhn): A large farm, often in a hot place, that grows mainly one type of crop

predator (PRED-uh-ter): An animal that hunts other animals for food

prehistoric (pree-hi-STAWR-ik): Belonging to a period in time before written history

scent marking (sent MAHR-king): A behavior by some animals in which they use scents produced by their bodies to communicate with other animals

snorkel (SNAWR-kuhl): A curved tube that allows a swimmer to breathe while underwater

snout (snout): The long or protruding part of the faces of some animals, consisting of the nose, mouth, and jaw

species (SPEE-sheez): A group of living things that are very similar and can have babies together

succulents (SUHK-yuh-luhnts): Plants that store water in their leaves or stems, helping them live in dry places

vegetation (vej-i-TEY-shuhn): Plant life

vulnerable (VUHL-ner-uh-buhl): An animal or plant species considered to be at high risk of extinction in the wild

wean (ween): When a young animal starts to eat food other than its mother's milk

INDEX

1. The Malayan tapir is a distant relative of the ______.
   a. horse
   b. elephant
   c. giant anteater

2. True or False: Malayan tapirs have 14 toes.

3. True or False: Both the Malayan tapir and the mountain tapir live in Asia.

4. Of all its senses, the Malayan tapir relies most on its sense of ______.
   a. sight
   b. smell
   c. touch

5. True or False: Malayan tapirs live in large groups called herds.

6. Malayan tapirs live for about ____ years.
   a. 10
   b. 20
   c. 30

7. A Malayan tapir calf weighs about ________ when it is born.
   a. 7 pounds (3 kg)
   b. 15 pounds (7 kg)
   c. 30 pounds (14 kg)

8. True or False: Malayan tapirs are most active at dawn and dusk.

ANSWERS
1. a, 2. True, 3. False, 4. b,
5. False, 6. c, 7. b, 8. True

About the Author

Annette Whipple is the author of many children's books, including *The Laura Ingalls Wilder Companion: A Chapter-by-Chapter Guide, Whooo Knew? The Truth About Owls, and Quirky Critter Devotions: 52 Wild Wonders for Kids.* When Annette's not reading or writing, you might find her baking for her family in Pennsylvania. Get to know her at AnnetteWhipple.com.

Written by: Annette Whipple

Editor: Ellen Rodger

Proofreader: Melissa Boyce

Design and layout: Tammy McGarr

Production manager: Candice Campbell

Image Credits

Shutterstock: Syahtuah Mohamed p 14, mangosteen p 21 (top), Punyaphat Larpsomboon p 39 (bottom), Arief Budi Kusuma p 40

Wikimedia Commons: Creative Commons p 5, © CEphoto, Uwe Aranas p 41

All other images from Shutterstock

Crabtree Publishing

crabtreebooks.com **800-387-7650**

Hardcover 978-1-0398-7482-4
Paperback 978-1-0398-8436-6
Ebook (pdf) 978-1-0398-8195-2
Epub 978-1-0398-8315-4

Published in Canada
Crabtree Publishing
616 Welland Avenue
St. Catharines, Ontario
L2M 5V6

Published in the United States
Crabtree Publishing
347 Fifth Avenue
Suite 1402-145
New York, New York, 10016

Library and Archives Canada Cataloguing in Publication
Available at Library and Archives Canada

Library of Congress Cataloging-in-Publication Data
Available at the Library of Congress

Printed in the U.S.A./CP022026